BEING CHURCH
IN THE NEW
MILLENNIUM

Department of Theological Questions
Irish Inter-Church Meeting

BEING CHURCH
IN THE NEW
MILLENNIUM

A Discussion Document

VERITAS

First published 2000 by
Veritas Publications
7-8 Lower Abbey Street
Dublin 1

ISBN 1 85390 384 1

British Library Cataloguing
in Publication Data.
A catalogue record for
this book is available
from the British Library.

Cover design by Barbara Croatto
Printed in the Republic of Ireland by Betaprint Ltd, Dublin

The Catholic Church in Ireland
The Church of Ireland
The Coptic Orthodox Church in Ireland
The Greek Orthodox Church in Britain and Ireland
LifeLink Network of Churches
The Methodist Church in Ireland
The Presbyterian Church in Ireland
The Non-Subscribing Presbyterian Church
The Moravian Church in Ireland
The Lutheran Church in Ireland
The Religious Society of Friends
The Salvation Army

The views expressed in this document do not necessarily represent those of the Irish Inter-Church Meeting or its Member Churches.

The Irish Inter-Church Meeting
Inter-Church Centre
48 Elmwood Avenue
Belfast BT9 6AZ

March 1999

CONTENTS

INTRODUCTION

Through the 1990s the Department of Theological Questions has been exploring theologically the challenges that the Churches face in a rapidly changing society. In *Freedom, Justice and Responsibility in Ireland Today* (1997), these challenges were placed in the context of the values of freedom, justice and responsibility.

In this current study document the Department is looking at being Church at the close of the twentieth century as we enter a new millennium. The aim is to encourage people to reflect on what being Church means and what it might mean.

There have been huge changes in Irish society over the past three decades and the stable religious worlds we have known for over a hundred years are now breaking up. The first discussion paper looks at the changes in Irish society over the last thirty years, the changes in the Churches, and the interaction between the two.

The second paper looks at models and types of Church – both at a general and a local level. The aim is to encourage reflection on what being Church meant and means.

The next four papers have been written by members of the Department from different traditions and deal with various aspects of being Church, for example:

- moving from a 'dispensing' to a 'seeking' Church;
- proclaiming a gospel rather than offering an option;
- having a relationship with Jesus Christ but also living with provisionality;
- diversity and development in the Church, and their limits;
- exploring the unity and continuity of faith;
- examining the nature of Christian discipleship and the rediscovery of commitment.

- rethinking priorities and resources;
- the Church as body of Christ;
- the Church as pilgrim people;
- the Church as a public community;
- the Church as a community of reconciling people;
- the Church as community of authentic transformation;
- the Church as ecumenical community.

The final paper deals with images of Church – particularly biblical images – in the belief that these may help us as we move into the future.

Of course, underlying discussion about being Church are theological questions. What is the purpose of the Church? Is it to solve the world's political and social problems? Is it to proclaim that 'here we have no lasting city?' Is it to proclaim the good news of Jesus Christ to a sinful world? Is it to be God's instrument in the eradication of enmity and the reconciliation of human division and hatred? Is it to be a sign and foretaste of the Kingdom of God? Is it to be a servant Church whose presence and power should be active in the world, bringing hope and strength to those who are suffering and oppressed? The World Council of Churches' Commission on Faith and Order paper 181, *The Nature and Purpose of the Church: A Stage on the Way to a Common Statement* (November 1998), deals with many of these issues (the Roman Catholic Church is a full member of the Commission). They are not, however, the primary focus of the present document.

Between the Churches there are significant differences in ecclesiology (the Church's institutional dimension). Churches differ according to where they perceive authority to lie, how decisions are made, and so on. These differences are important. Again, they are not the focus of the present study document.

Increasingly, the understanding has developed that the Church is not primarily an institutional or organisational reality with a constitution, a set of rules, a governing body, a set of actual members, etc. Of course, these external, visible features of the Church are important, but they are not of her essence. Most of the material in this study document seeks in various ways to reflect on this reality.

Question
1. How do you answer the question: What is the purpose of the Church?

I

IRISH SOCIETY AND THE CHURCH

Dr David Stevens

Churches are profoundly affected by the society of which they are part. In turn, they also influence society. This paper seeks to get us thinking about the society we inhabit and the reality of being Church in Ireland today. It had its origin in an exercise carried out by the members of the Department.

The paper is not offered in a spirit of condemning the world (Jn 3:17), nor to induce pessimism in the Churches. The world remains God's world and God is at work in it. Religion still plays a substantial part in the lives of people in Ireland, both North and South. What we are seeking to provide is a reality check and a stimulus for reflection about Irish society, the Church, and the relationship between the two.

The following points are not offered as a complete picture. They may be caricatures, or over-simplistic; some statements may contradict others.

- The pervasiveness and power of the media, particularly television – ours is an image-centred culture.
- Globalisation: integration into the global economy and culture of McDonalds, Coca Cola and jeans; exposure to new ideas and influences; foreign travel; new information technologies.
- The increasing speed of technological change.
- Economic growth has become the national priority.
- Changing work and employment patterns: more women working, less security in employment.

- The move from a predominantly rural to a predominantly urban society.
- A more fragmented and complex society.
- Increasing mobility; many people no longer live most of their lives in small localised communities.
- Loss of community in some places.
- Changing patterns of family life; rise in number of single parents, increase in cohabitation, large-scale marital breakdown.
- A revolution in sexual mores.
- The changing role of women; the 'gender revolution'.
- People living longer, often retiring earlier.
- The emergence of a youth-orientated culture.
- The importance of consumerism, pleasure dominance, worship of success, competitive individualism.
- Changing patterns of leisure and entertainment; the importance of sport; the rise in interest in personal fitness and well-being.
- Increasing pressures on people: to succeed; on time; in relationships; in work.
- Marked intensification of social competitiveness, in the workplace, in the economy and in the education system.
- Increasing levels of educational attainment.
- Growing prosperity along with a more unequal society and the reality of the significant number of people who have been excluded from the mainstream.
- A more diverse Ireland; the presence of ethnic minorities, refugees, asylum-seekers, etc.
- The effects of violence and political division in Northern Ireland.
- A less stable and secure and more provisional and uncertain world – we are living in 'times of dislocation' (Walter Brueggemann).
- An emphasis on personal freedom and autonomy.

- The importance of personal relations and intimacy.
- The importance of personal authenticity; hatred of hypocrisy.
- Hunger for community among some.
- Sensitivity among some to victimised groups and to justice issues.
- An emphasis on inclusiveness and tolerance.
- Concern for the environment.
- A search for personal meaning and identity.
- A search for spirituality, but often dissociated from clearly defined belief systems or corporate loyalties.
- Many people's sense/reality of pain and hurt and the rise of 'therapies'.
- Move from a culture of obedience into one of experience.
- The search for new experiences, for example, drugs.
- The suspicion of authority: political, Church, etc.
- The valuing of newness over tradition.
- An age of exposure and openness.
- Developing pluralism in Irish society, where there is no common understanding about values.
- Values and beliefs increasingly a matter of choice, less a matter of tradition.
- Traditional values that once were lived as public values are today being privatised.
- 'Post-modern' denial of meaning and rejection of absolutes.
- People shopping around for their answers to moral and religious questions – the 'pick-and-mix' society.
- People decide 'what is true for me'; we now inhabit a world of options and preferences.
- Difficulty with long-term and exclusive commitments.
- The importance of the 'here and now'.
- Increasing number of people living their lives without reference to religious beliefs.

- Decline in Mass and church attendance.
- No longer a sense of 'the all-embracing story' which gives meaning to life.
- Growing lack of connection between religious belief and everyday living.
- Privatisation of religious belief.
- Failure of Churches to help people make sense of a changing world.
- Loss of transcendence; God gets drowned out in busyness; there is no ultimate meaning, etc.
- Growing sense among some people that the Church is an oppressive reality, seeking to tell people how to live their lives and limit their freedom.
- Gap between those for whom the world of Church remains nourishing and those for whom it has become empty and even incredible.
- Disappearance of cultural and institutional support systems for a faith stance.
- The anger of many women with the Church.
- Decline in number of clergy and religious in Roman Catholic Church.
- The loss of authority of the Churches over the last thirty years.
- The Churches' decline in institutional influence.
- The association of Churches with national identity: Britishness, Irishness.
- Sectarianism and communal division, and the association of the Churches with them.
- The role of religion as a source of conflict in Northern Ireland.
- Changes in how parishes/congregations relate to the local community.
- The rise of secular organisations providing welfare services, youth work, etc.

- Greater contact and co-operation between Churches.
- The Church as bulwark against change for some – a safe space in a rapidly changing world.
- Growing diversity within mainstream Churches.
- The conservative/liberal split within Northern Ireland Protestantism.
- Growing separation of Church from certain groups in society, for example, urban poor.
- People's search for vibrancy of worship, spiritual depth, real commitment and community, and the challenge that this represents for existing Church cultures.
- Rise of new religious groups.
- Weakening denominational loyalties, the religious supermarket.

Questions
1. Which of these statements do you recognise as valid? Tick as appropriate.
2. How has society changed over the last thirty years?
3. How has this affected the Churches?
4. How has the Church changed?
5. What would you regard as the main strengths and weaknesses of the Churches and Church life in Ireland today?
6. How does your Church relate to the society/local community around it?
7. Does your congregation/parish care about what is happening round about the doors of the church?
8. Do you and your congregation/parish live in an enclosed 'churchy' world?

II

MODELS AND TYPES OF CHURCH

Dr David Stevens

The purpose of this paper is to encourage reflection on models and types of Church. The following are offered for consideration.

At a general level

- The Christendom model of Church. Christianity is the glue that binds society together. The Church normally supports established authority and is institutionally influential; Church and society are almost co-extensive; the Church accepts responsibility for society and seeks to act as its conscience.
- Church as contrast community, as counter-culture; an alternative to the existing social order, having a different and distinct ethic; a Church witnessing at the margins.
- A 'public Church' in conversation with the wider society.
- A servanthood model of Church: the Churches as servants of society.
- A dispensing model of Church, dispensing truth, grace, the sacraments, the word, welfare services, education, etc., ministering to the needs of individuals who present themselves (see Paper III).
- Church as teacher of faith.
- Church as community of learning: helping each person to become a 'humble learner in the school of Christ'.
- Church as sacrament – as God's sign and agent in the world.

- Church as the assembly of believers among whom the word of God is faithfully preached.
- Church as the invisible community of the saved.
- Church as visible, historical institution and reality.
- Church as hierarchical authority.
- Church as community of disciples.
- Church as voluntary community.
- Church as part of an ethnic minority/national community; the Church of the people – the Irish, Scots and English at prayer.
- Church as international and universal community.
- Church as local gathering of those who have professed their faith in Jesus Christ.

At the local level

- The gathered (associational) Church of people who may come from a wide area, and who share common theological convictions or 'churchmanship'; Church/community boundaries are clear; may offer a substitute community with a full range of social activities.
- The communal Church whose members have an implicitly shared idea about their parish as community, for which they have some responsibility; membership local and diverse in background; Church/community boundaries are blurred, the parish tying 'civil and social life together with religious faith and community identity' (Fintan O'Toole).
- The competitive Church: seeking to generate loyalty, identity and numbers over and against the rival claims of other local Churches; emphasises differences from other Churches; often seeks to become a self-contained society; operates particularly in a community that contains a variety of different religious groups.

Questions
1. What do you consider the present model(s) of Church to be: in your area? in your denomination? in general?
2. What were they in your childhood?
3. How ought the Church relate to the local community?
4. How ought the Church relate to society?

III

FORWARD TO THE PAST
– A CHURCH FOR THE FUTURE?

Very Rev. Dr Stephen White

There has been much discussion – both within the Department of Theological Questions and outside it – about the ways in which Church and society are changing rapidly, and about the ways in which the Church can hope most effectively to continue to speak to that changed society.

The Church and the challenge of a changing society

Of all the changes that have occurred during the last two or three generations in society and in the general world-view of many people, there are two in particular that have profound implications for the life and witness of the Church, both in the present and in the future.

Firstly, society – and with it people's cultural, philosophical and religious outlook – has become increasingly pluralist and relativist. There is an astonishing array of options from which to choose, as cultures, religions and traditions intermingle. No longer do I have to follow (largely through the lack of any alternative) the pattern in which I was brought up. I have only to look around to see that there are many ways and values upon which I may choose – choose being the operative word – to build my life. Or I may elect to take what I perceive to be the best features of several options and create my own personal belief and/or value system, one that works for me.

Secondly, and as a direct corollary both of this fact and of the continuous and rapid strides in scientific and technological discovery, society has become at once more forward-looking and more provisional. Just as a scientist holds a particular theory at any one time – but one that is always acknowledged to be entirely provisional, awaiting replacement if a better theory with greater explanatory potential becomes available – so too any ethical, philosophical or religious standpoint is perceived as provisional. It may possibly be binding for the present, but it is not immune to new influences and is not so sacrosanct that it cannot be changed or even abandoned in the light of events or experiences.

If these features of pluralism, relativism and provisionality reflect at all accurately the face of society today, then presumably the Church that ministers to and witnesses in such a climate needs to be one that is capable of responding to these trends in society – not, it should be stressed, to the extent of being subsumed by them or selling out to them, but rather by acknowledging that they are real and need to be addressed in the Church's manner of life and proclamation.

Thus the question immediately arises: Is the Church of today, in any of its denominational forms, capable of rising to the challenge of such a world and speaking credibly to it?

Dogma and doctrine

My personal answer to this question is that it is not. In all of its forms, from the most fundamentalist sect through to the mainstream denominations, the Church is in one way or another dogma-centred. I use the word 'dogma' rather than 'doctrine' advisedly, as there is a world of difference between the two. Where doctrine is essential and has a definite function, dogma is prone to petrifaction and can kill the life it seeks to foster. Furthermore, I am aware that I may well be using the words 'doctrine' and 'dogma' in a sense that is somewhat different from that which may be used by some people. Thus 'dogma' (which I am using in a pejorative sense) may be spoken of in some circles as being creative and as being, broadly, a synonym for 'doctrine'.

However, I feel nonetheless that the two terms need to be separated more widely than is often the case, for they represent in essence two ways of thinking, one creative and one possessive.

First, doctrine. Doctrine is, in my understanding of the term, a creative human response to our perceptions of the divine revelation – 'our perceptions' because there is not, and never can be, any such thing as a divine revelation that is entirely objective or unfiltered through the medium of the human consciousness. As soon as I encounter divinity (however directly and apparently objectively), I encounter it as a human being, and my perceptions are always, therefore, coloured by my humanity, with its failings and imperfections. Doctrine, then, is the attempt to make sense, to the best of our limited ability, of our glimpses of God: to give shape, form and defining expression to an encounter and a reality that is, by its very nature, ultimately beyond us, and therefore beyond any verbal expression that we can give to it.

There is, therefore, a 'provisionality' about doctrine, however concrete it might seem. We perceive God – or any facet of God's activity – in such and such a way, but there is always the possibility (however remote it may seem to us at the time) that this perception may be inadequate or even wrong and may need to be reformulated or even revised entirely in the light of a subsequent and greater understanding. Thus, in the nature of doctrine, questioning and testing of received opinion are not destructive or threatening, still less heretical. They are a privilege, and indeed an obligation, as we seek to gain the fullest possible understanding of the God whom we meet and worship – and nothing less than total openness to the ever-new possibility of revelation is sufficient by way of our own self-giving in response. Our most cherished human formulations must always remain provisional in the presence of the ultimate mystery that is God.

By contrast, what I have defined as 'dogma' is the petrifaction of doctrine. It is the clinging to familiar shibboleths or patterns of belief in order to ward off the possibility – or threat – that these may be inadequate. It is a deification of human formulations at the expense of the reality of God. It is, in effect, a closing of a door that God may be trying to open a little further. It is ourselves saying to God, 'This is who you are', and not allowing God to lead us into the 'fullness of truth' by enabling us to understand something new about divine nature. In a nutshell, 'I believe in God' is doctrine: 'I believe in God the Father' may become dogma if it leads us to ignore the feminine and become locked into a paternalistic and misogynistic understanding of either faith or Church.

The dispensing Church

The basic self-understanding of the Church – which it has had for a very long time and which, it must be admitted, has worked for most of that period! – is that the Church is the guardian of the repository of all truth in the form of those propositions that we are required to believe for our salvation, and that this truth can in some way be 'dispensed' to those who come within its orbit. Christianity is not so much about finding anything out – either about ourselves or about God – as about being told what has already been found out and then being required to believe it! If this is an accurate sketch of the Church's fundamental self-understanding, then it is hardly surprising that Church and society should be drifting apart, with the Church as the loser.

The seeking Church

If, then, a 'dispensing' Church is not adequate, what model of Church might we coherently propose for the present, and – even more importantly – for the future? The word I have come to use to describe this Church is the 'seeking' church. And it is important that it is a Church and a seeking that is based on relationship: a relationship with God through Jesus Christ.

Such a Church has links – and a real continuity – with the early Church in a way that a 'dispensing' Church has not. There is no space here to do justice to the idea, but one receives the powerful impression both from the New Testament and from the non-canonical works of the sub-apostolic era, that most of the authors are wrestling with the impact of Jesus and trying to understand what relationship with him and with the fullness of the Trinitarian God might mean in terms of worship, Church order, lifestyle, ethics, etc. And in this discussion there is – on non-essentials – much room for manoeuvre. All would agree that certain actions and attitudes are, or are not, worthy of a Christian. However, there is, as yet, no hard and fast requirement to subscribe to one particular interpretation of events: the Virgin Birth or not – St Mark, St John and St Paul show no interest in it; atonement – no one theory has command; no one has yet set in concrete the relationship of human and divine in Jesus; and so on and so on! All of these authors, it appears, are simply seeking to respond to and elucidate the impact and implications of Jesus Christ for themselves and their readers in a way that combines certainty and openness.

Again, there is insufficient space to allow for detail, but here, perhaps, is a model for today. Clearly, if the Church is to remain recognisably the Church and still have 'a gospel to proclaim', rather than merely 'an option to offer', it needs to retain some degree of certainty. Perhaps, however, this certainty can be located – as I believe it ultimately was for the early Church – in the person of Jesus Christ and in his revelation of God, rather than in specific dogmatic formulations.

Doctrine, as we have said, is important: so, for example, doctrine may proclaim that Jesus Christ is the Son of God. Beyond this, which is more important? That someone should have a living relationship with God through Jesus Christ or that they assent to a particular understanding of that sonship or of his atoning sacrifice?

If Jesus Christ becomes again the focus of our Christian living and worship, perhaps we can then be a seeking Church – seeking to know him – which can draw in all who would seek, at whatever level, for truth. We know that we have the certainty of truth in him so far as we can perceive it, and yet we are also able to acknowledge, at every stage on the way, the provisionality of our current understanding of that truth. Faith, then, also becomes a journey and a search, to which anyone may be invited or which anyone may feel free to join without any prior preconditions. A willingness to seek is all.

The Church's potential for error

Such a relaxation and withdrawal from any claim to absolute understanding or authority makes possible a more open approach, which has liberating consequences for us. If our doctrine is only that – our doctrine – and not the absolute guaranteed truth about God and about every aspect of God's will, then in view of our human frailty, we may realistically expect ourselves to be mistaken from time to time. We may even turn out to have been mistaken not merely on minor matters of interpretation but on issues of real substance that have had major repercussions on the lives of men and women.

This potential for error is a curious case of what sounds initially like bad news turning out to be good news, especially for a Church that is committed to an honest and open seeking for God. It is good news because we may reasonably expect that what we know about ourselves – that is, our propensity to well-intentioned error – God also knows. We may assume that God 'expects' these mistakes and that actions and understandings undertaken 'in good faith' are not culpable even if their consequences turn out to be undesirable. If this is the case, then we are freed to have a more relaxed attitude towards our own thinking. We are set free to be creative and open to experimentation as we seek to understand God and his will for us, expecting not God's condemnation of our wrongdoing, but his understanding and forgiveness of our inevitable errors as we grapple with so much that is at the limits of – and indeed not infrequently beyond – our comprehension.

Our understanding represents the limits of our seeking today; yet, for the future, it is only a living relationship with Jesus Christ – and a continued devout and open seeking of him – that will lead us into more of the truth. About our knowledge of the truth, though not about its existence, we are content to remain – as we must – provisional.

Questions
1. In what ways can the Church rise to the challenge of a world characterised by pluralism, relativism and provisionality?
2. In what ways is there a 'provisionality' about doctrine in the sense in which the doctrine is understood in the text? Must all human formulations remain provisional in the presence of the ultimate mystery that is God?
3. In what ways does today's Church correspond to the dispensing Church model?
4. How would a 'seeking' Church based on a living relationship with Jesus Christ be an alternative?
5. What must we be committed to and have certainty about in the Christian faith and what can remain provisional?
6. What are the implications for the Church when she acknowledges that she has got something wrong?

IV

UNITY AND DIVERSITY IN THE CHURCH

Most Rev. Dr Leo O'Reilly

The starting point of this Paper is a statement in Paper III:

> Clearly, if the Church is to remain recognisably the
> Church and still have 'a gospel to proclaim' rather than
> merely 'an option to offer', it needs to retain some degree
> of certainty. Perhaps, however, this certainty can be
> located… in the person of Jesus Christ and in his
> revelation of God, rather than in specific dogmatic
> formulations.

It is clear that whatever certainty the Church claims *must* be
located in the person of Jesus Christ. Jesus is the *raison d'être* of
the Church. The Church exists to proclaim his message and to
continue his ministry in the world. We can go even further and
say that Jesus himself is the message that the Church preaches.
The word that the Church preaches is the Word made Flesh who
lived among us: 'We declare to you what was from the beginning,
what we have heard, what we have seen with our eyes . . .
concerning the word of life – this life was revealed, and we have
seen it and testify to it…' (1 Jn 1:1-2). So it is not just Jesus'
message that is the object of the Church's preaching, it is the
person of Jesus himself.

Who do people say that I am?

However, locating our certainty in the person of Jesus Christ is
not as simple as it seems. We sometimes hear people say, when

faced with a moral dilemma or indeed a decision of any kind:
What would Jesus do in these circumstances? The question
supposes that the person asking it is in a position to know with
certainty what Jesus would do, and this, presumably, on the basis
that they know the mind of Jesus and, therefore, Jesus himself.
But even in Jesus' own day there were many different views about
his identity. At the turning point in his ministry he asked his
disciples: 'Who do people say that I am?' Peter quotes a variety
of current opinions, but is asked more pointedly, 'Who do you
say I am?' The answer to this question clearly takes for granted
the obvious human identity of Jesus. Jesus' question refers to the
deeper mystery of his person, and the answer, as the Gospel of
Matthew makes explicit, is a confession of faith: 'Flesh and blood
has not revealed this to you, but my Father who is in heaven'
(16:17). However, apart from the erroneous opinions, there are
different answers in the different Gospels, and that suggests that
even within the New Testament there was a development in the
understanding of the identity of Jesus. In St Mark the answer was
'The Christ', in Luke 'The Christ of God', and in Matthew 'The
Christ the Son of the living God'. St John's Gospel goes
considerably further when it puts on the lips of Thomas the
confession of Jesus as 'My Lord and my God'.

Diversity in understandings of Jesus

The different titles given to Jesus in the New Testament represent
a diversity in the understanding of who he was and in the
interpretation of his significance. There is also a clear
development in the expression of what Jesus meant to the early
Church, if not in the actual understanding of what he meant.
The high Christology of St John's Gospel ('My Lord and my
God') is certainly not explicit in St Mark, if it is there at all.
However, it is becoming explicit in St Matthew, as we see from
his redaction of Mark 6:45-52: 'And those in the boat
worshipped him, saying, "Truly you are the Son of God"'

(cf. Mt 28:17). So while there is diversity there is also development, but this diversity and development are contained within the unity of the New Testament canon, which lays down the parameters within which the person of Jesus is to be correctly understood.

We know that this process of reflection on the identity of Jesus continued in the centuries that followed and that the results of that reflection were expressed in the formulations of the Councils of Nicaea and Chalcedon. The doctrinal formulations of Nicaea and Chalcedon were arrived at only after protracted and often rancorous debate. These dogmatic definitions do not replace Christ as the object of our faith, but they do have an important role in preserving the integrity of our faith in Christ. They were designed with only one purpose in mind, namely, to ensure that the question, 'Who do people say I am?', continued to be answered correctly in the Church. If we take seriously the words of Jesus: 'Eternal life is this: to know you the one true God and Jesus Christ whom you have sent' (Jn 17:3), then being sure about who Jesus is, is a matter of the utmost importance for Christians.

Unity and continuity of faith

We see, therefore, that if one of the fundamental tasks of the Church is to preach Christ, then it must be agreed on who Christ is. That is, there must be unity of faith. In the period preceding the Second Vatican Council, the positions of the Catholic and Protestant Churches on what was the rule of faith were polarised. Catholics appealed to tradition as proclaimed by the teaching authority of the Church, the Magisterium. Protestants looked to Scripture alone – *sola scriptura* – as the rule of faith. However, the document *Dei verbum* of the Council heralded a shift in emphasis in the Catholic position. While reaffirming the role of the teaching office of the Church, the document states immediately afterwards:

> This teaching office is not above the word of God, but serves it, teaching only what has been handed on, listening to it devoutly, guarding it scrupulously, and explaining it faithfully by divine commission and with the help of the Holy Spirit.[1]

The polarisation meant that in Catholic thinking and practice there was a tendency to overrate the importance of 'tradition' at the expense of Scripture, with a consequent exaggeration of the role of the Magisterium. In Protestant thinking, the *sola scriptura* principle could be employed to justify any individual's interpretation of the sacred text, with a consequent tendency to fragmentation into different denominations. However, the Protestant position is much more nuanced than a literal translation of *sola scriptura* would suggest. For Anglicans, the emphasis in the understanding of revelation is upon Scripture, Reason and Tradition taken together as the norm of interpretation. As far back as 1963, the Faith and Order Conference in Montreal concluded that:

> the opposition between 'Scripture' and 'Tradition', as it has been known to us since the sixteenth century as the subject of the controversy, appears as a marginal problem.[2]

Unity and continuity of faith were major concerns of the primitive Church as well as of our own. St Paul's concern for unity of faith in the crucial matter of the Resurrection prompts him to appeal to what had been 'handed on': 'For I handed on to you as of first importance what I in turn had received: that Christ died for our sins . . .' (1 Cor 15:3). St Paul appeals to the same process of handing on in relation to Eucharistic faith: 'For I received from the Lord what I also handed on to you, that the Lord Jesus on the night when he was betrayed . . .' (1 Cor 11:23). St Paul was writing at a time when our distinction between

Scripture and Tradition did not exist. The scriptural canon had not yet been completed and the contents of 'tradition', like creeds and liturgical rites, were still in the making. Paul is referring to a more fundamental *traditio* or 'handing on', of which the Church itself is the subject. The Second Vatican Council, in its decree *Dei verbum,* has recovered this earlier understanding of tradition:

> The Church, in her teaching, life and worship, perpetuates and hands on to all generations all that she herself is, all that she believes.[3]

Karl Rahner explains more fully what 'tradition' in this wider sense means:

> In the comprehensive sense, therefore, tradition is not primarily a 'something', an objectified datum. It is not exclusively, when taken in its full sense, either the transmission of the word of God in Scripture or the handing on of truths and forms of piety not committed to writing. It is the faith of the Church in action, which is more than its expression in propositions both because Christ works in this faith and because not all that is done in faith is adequately accessible to reflection and expression. For this reason too, the living faith of the Church is also the ultimate norm for criticism of tradition within the Church.[4]

Knowing Jesus

Returning now to the question of Jesus, 'Who do people say that I am?', and the problem of ensuring that this question continues to be answered correctly in every generation, we recognise that it is much more than a question of passing on information about Jesus, or ensuring that the right words are used when speaking about him. Both Scripture and tradition (in the narrow sense) are important for nourishing our faith in Jesus and in helping us to know who he is. But we must go beyond knowing who he is to knowing him personally. 'And this is eternal life, that they may know you, the only true God, and Jesus Christ whom you have sent' (Jn 17:3). To know in the biblical sense is to enter into a relationship with someone, and so the task of the Church is to enable people to enter into a relationship with Jesus Christ. It should enable them to experience the love of Christ in their lives and to respond to that love. The Church's role, then, is not just to pass on knowledge about Jesus but to make him present and active in the lives of its members. It does this through the process of Tradition, in the wider sense used by the Second Vatican Council, that of handing on 'all that she herself is, all that she believes'.[5]

The Church as the Body of Christ

The model of the Church that seems most suited to encompassing this understanding of the Church as an active subject in history (handing on all that she is) and at the same time as a community with diverse ministries and charisms, is the Church as the body of Christ. This model is well attested in the New Testament: 'Now you are the body of Christ and individually members of it' (1 Cor 12:27; cf. 1 Cor 12:12f); 'He is the head of the body, the church' (Col 1:18; cf. Eph 1:23). The model of the Church as the body of Christ has the advantage that it holds together the diverse elements in the Church in a unity rooted in the Holy Spirit (1 Cor 12:4f). The Church is a community of diverse members and activities, but it is united under one head, and it acts as one subject who is Christ. We conclude, therefore, that Christ is both the subject and the object of the Church's activity. He is what is handed on and he is the one who hands it on. Christ is the head of the Church and also its foundation and cornerstone. The Church is essentially christological in nature.

The understanding of the Church as the body of Christ might appear at first sight to be light years removed from the mindsets of the consumerist secular world we live in. How can such a seemingly arcane theological construct help us to speak to a world in which the defining characteristics are relativism, materialism, individualism and all the other 'isms' that we associate with the post-modern age? How can such a Church speak to the modern world in a way that its voice will be heard and understood?

Evangelisation and witness

The key to evangelisation today is surely witness. People of our time are more impressed by witness than by teachers, and if they listen to the latter it is because they also bear witness.[6] Witness is what makes the body of Christ visible in the world. If the Church is going to make Christ present in the world it must become more and more what it is, the body of Christ. In other words, it must embody Christ, embody his love, his compassion, and his forgiveness, in short, his life. *And this means that the Church must be united in love as well as in faith.* Few, if any, come to faith in Christ through intellectual enquiry alone. People are much more likely to come to faith through the experience of Christianity lived and practised in an authentic and caring Christian community. Such a community embodies Christ in a way that makes his presence felt as something liberating and life-giving. The word becomes flesh in the lives of loving and committed followers of Jesus. This is the most powerful form of evangelisation because it combines word and witness. It fulfils the promise of Jesus to his disciples: 'By this everyone will know that you are my disciples, if you have love for one another' (Jn 13:35).

References

1. *Documents of Vatican II*, (ed.) Walter Abbot (1996), par. 10.
2. *The Common Catechism*, (eds.) Johannes Feiner and Lukas Vischer (London: Search Press, 1975), p. 564.3. *Documents of Vatican II*, (ed.) Walter Abbot (1996), par. 8.
4. *Encyclopedia of Theology, A Concise Sacramentum Mundi*, (ed.) Karl Rahner (London: Burns and Oates, 1975), p. 1730.
5. *Documents of Vatican II*, (ed.) Walter Abbot (1996), par. 8.
6. Pope Paul VI, *Evangelisation in the Modern World* (London: Catholic Truth Society, 1975), p. 41.

Questions
1. 'It must be agreed on who Christ is. That is, there must be unity of faith.' How is the unity and continuity of faith to be maintained in a pluralistic age?
2. 'The Church's role is not just to pass on knowledge about Jesus but to make him present and active in the lives of its members.' How is this to be done today?
3. How can an understanding of the Church as the body of Christ 'speak to a world in which the defining characteristics are relativism, materialism, individualism and the other 'isms' that we associate with the post-modern age'?
4. The key to evangelisation (evangelism) today is witness. How valid is this statement?
5. 'People are much more likely to come to faith through the experience of Christianity lived and practised in an authentic and caring Christian community.' How can we create (or be given) such communities?

V

COMMITMENT AND THE CHURCH

Rev. Dr Trevor Morrow

One of the striking features of the contemporary Church scene is the lack of commitment. In spite of the ever-increasing number of Church organisations and ministries, it is becoming increasingly difficult to find anyone to service them. In parts of the island, where tribal allegiance is still strong, there is still a great sense of loyalty to the local Church community, if only to wave the correct flag and to show clearly what we are not. However, the combination of individualism and consumerism means that the Church is treated more like a restaurant or supermarket than as an essential expression of a person's identity. Membership is not only declining but those who remain are often merely conforming to the required obligations, and only when absolutely necessary. Unless we rediscover the nature of Christian discipleship, those in leadership will be a gathering of officers without an army.

Commitment and the ministry of Jesus

The ministry of Jesus was characterised by an appeal for radical commitment. His expectations were that to follow him would be at enormous cost (Lk 9:23-24). For the first disciples this involved an immediate and physical interaction with Jesus, who used the rabbinical model of instruction. Since the message of Jesus and the person of Jesus were inseparable, the commitment involved was to him as well to his ministry.

Luke 9:57-62 tells of three incidents where Jesus relates to potential disciples. The first man wants to be part of the action but his understanding of discipleship appears shallow. Jesus' response in terms of the security of foxes and birds over and against the Son of Man may involve the use of political symbolism. T. W. Manson points out that birds and foxes were apocalyptic symbols for the gentile nations. He writes:

> Then the sense of the saying may be: everybody is at home in Israel's land except the true Israel. The birds of the air – the Roman overlords, the foxes – the Edomite interlopers, have made their position secure. The true Israel is disinherited by them: And if you cast your lot with me and mine you join the ranks of the dispossessed and you must be prepared to serve God under those conditions.[1]

The second would-be disciple does not volunteer. He is recruited. His request to bury his father first seems reasonable. However, in the context of the Middle East, this request reflects a concern to fulfil the responsibility a son has to his father to care for him in his old age and restfully lay him in the grave. It is what social custom would demand. The man's request, therefore, reflects the social or peer pressure to conform to community expectations before a commitment to being a disciple of Jesus. The response of Jesus assumes that there will be confrontation with the social norms in living for his kingdom.

The third potential disciple brashly offers to follow the master. Jesus' pre-condition is that he takes leave of those at home. It seems rather severe that Jesus will not allow him even to say goodbye to his family. However, the early listeners and readers know that 'to take leave of' means to seek permission from his father to become a disciple. Everyone knows that this will be rejected. Being a disciple of Jesus means accepting no higher authority than Jesus himself. It is like ploughing with a light hand-plough. It requires a steady hand and a deliberate looking forward. If, says Jesus, you are looking around to see what your peers or even your family want, you cannot be my disciple.

The command to the Church is to make such disciples. Discipleship and baptism were for the early Church inseparable because it is in the Church as the body of Christ that we are discipled, through apostolic doctrine, fellowship, breaking of bread and prayer. We cannot be a disciple without radical commitment and we cannot be co-workers with Christ in the fulfilment of his mission unless we are his disciples.

Rethinking priorities and resources

The implications for the Church today is to rethink our priorities and resources. Most of our energies are channelled either into the maintenance of our institutional structures, which often perpetuate a nominal commitment mindset, or into moralistic mission, in which the pious few are guilt-driven to do more and more of what is believed to be the responsibility of the kingdom of God.

Let us not despair; the present downsizing of the Church is perhaps an act of a merciful God to enable us to rediscover Christian discipleship through radical commitment.

Grace and law

The tendency within us all is to respond to the need for radical commitment with the imposition of law. The Judaisers in Galatia were highly motivated and were concerned not merely with the preservation of their Jewish inheritance but with the moral and spiritual integrity of the faithful. Their insistence on the keeping of the law was to demonstrate who were the truly committed to the faith of their forebears. We, too, might easily resort to a strict sacramental discipline or a potentially two-tier membership of the Church in order to achieve the goal of a disciplined committed people. It would seem that the emphasis of Jesus and the apostles on Grace/Freedom/Commitment, in that order, would more effectively create authentic Christian discipleship. It is when we are set free by grace to be who we were made to be that we discover the paradox of faith – that in order to find myself, I have to lose myself in loving, which is self-giving. This is so antithetical to the spirit of the age and much of the psychobabble that dominates popular thought, that we are confronted with an enormous challenge. How do we communicate the heart of the faith as expressed by the sixteenth-century poet, Robert Southwell, 'Not when I breathe, but when I love, I live'? The answer to that question will produce radical committed disciples of Jesus Christ for the new millennium.

Reference

1. T. W. Manson, *The Sayings of Jesus* (London: SCM, 1937), p. 72.

Questions
1. In what ways is a lack of commitment evident in the present-day Church? Why is this so?
2. What makes commitment so difficult today? Were the Churches in previous generations simply part of the culture in which one lived, taken for granted with the social environment? In what ways have the cultural and institutional supports for faith commitment disappeared in Irish society? How can people live against the mainstream of modern culture?
3. In what ways are our Churches legalistic and moralistic faith communities?
4. All communities of shared faith and commitment are concerned with the moral formation of their members – the Church is a moral community. In the fragmented condition of a post-modern world, how can our Churches be effective communities of moral nurture?
5. Belonging to Christ means belonging to his body, the Church. How can we foster commitment to the Church?

VI

CHANGING MODELS OF THE CHURCH

Rev. Dr Johnston McMaster

The Church has faced challenges and issues in every age, and in every age and situation has had to proclaim and live out the gospel in different ways. There are always moments in history when shifts in thought-patterns, language, methods and style are required. At the end of the twentieth century we live in one of those moments. It is not a moment for retreat into defensive mode, still less behind immovable barricades. It is a time to journey and explore, to move forward into a very different world. Ireland, as part of that changing world, is not the same place it was twenty years ago. In the Republic of Ireland in particular, change has been rapid and radical. Though still struggling with the ancient quarrel, Northern Ireland is changing, and is now facing the possibility of a process of deep change. The potential for change over the next twenty years will not leave the ancient quarrel untouched. Context, therefore, is important because the Church does not live outside or above the social, political and cultural contexts. The Church is always in the world, though called to be a transformative presence and to embody alternative values and relationships.

At the end of the twentieth century, Ireland is more secular than it has been in its Christian history. Increasing numbers of people experience Church as a conservative and reactionary institution. For some, the experience of Church is oppressive. Traditional expressions of God-talk, faith and worship no longer connect with living experience. The role of the Church in society is diminishing, with less participation as of right in the structures of public power. The power of the Church in public and political life is not what it was twenty years ago. The level of faith practice and the relation of the Church to power structures are likely to continue to diminish. A political settlement contributing to a more stable society in Northern Ireland is likely to accelerate the decrease in Church attendance; that pattern was observed following the 1994 ceasefires. A changing context requires changing models of Church.

Peter Hodgson, both in *Winds of the Spirit* and *Revisioning the Church*, offers a definition of Ecclesial Community:

> Ecclesia is a transfigured mode of human community, an image of God's project for the world embodied in a diversity of historical churches, comprising a plurality of peoples and cultural traditions, founded upon the life, death and resurrection of Christ, created by the redemptive presence of God as spirit. It is a community in which privatistic, provincial and hierarchical modes of existence are challenged and being overcome, and in which is fragmentarily actualised a universal reconciling love that liberates from sin and death, alienation and oppression.[1]

The definition offers several pointers to the shape Church might take in a changing context:

(a)   The Church is the sign and agent of Jesus' vision of God's kingdom. The vision is of a community created by God and which expresses a new way of being communally human in the world;

(b)   There are four biblical images of Church that, though old, express the changing models required by the contemporary context. The images are people, body, communion, Spirit – all relational, communal, creative and dynamic;

(c)   The four classic marks of Church are present – one, holy, catholic and apostolic. They are also redefined in and for the contemporary world context. Unity is expressed in plurality. Holiness is expressed in a commitment to the world and all creation and is embodied in an alternative lifestyle. Catholicity overcomes the privatistic, provincial and hierarchical and is radically universal, while apostolicity is shaped by Christ-centred mission in and to the world, involving the personal and structural.

What models of Church, then, are required in Ireland at the end of the twentieth century?

1. Church as pilgrim people

This model relates to where increasing numbers of people are, consciously and unconsciously: seekers for meaning, relationships, connectedness and community. The institutional and theological package no longer appears to have the capacity to connect with seekers. Faith as packaged, to be accepted or rejected, is no longer where many are. Confessionalism, dogmas and doctrinal systems are not life-giving good news. This is not to say that theology is unimportant, but pilgrim people, on a journey, will do theology in a different key.

The sense of journeying, seeking and questing applies equally to evangelisation and spirituality. Evangelists and soul friends are fellow-travellers, indeed often wounded travellers. The invitation to journey with friends will have more contemporary resonance than the dispensing of institutionalised grace, however well packaged.

2. Church as public community

Churches have lived out of the Christendom model. Even if not constitutionally or officially State Churches, the larger denominations have developed a Constantinian praxis, closely related to systems and structures of power. The model is collapsing, and Ireland is no exception. This means a new and very different model of being public Church.

It will mean moving beyond the privatised or individualistic model of faith to faith that is public, social and political. A social reading of Scripture and expression of liturgy and service are required.

This will not mean the Church trying to re-establish itself or attempting once again to dominate social and political structures, but faith lived out in service within the marketplace. Service rather than dominance will be key, but this will move social ministry beyond works of charity and philanthropy to ministries of justice. Caring and justice in the public place will include charity and action for systemic change or structural reform. And these are the responsibility and calling of all the people of God.

3. Church as community of reconciling dialogue

The contemporary context in which faith is lived is multi-faceted. The myth of a monochrome Irish culture, even a pure Irish culture, has been exploded. Even talk of two cultural traditions in Northern Ireland has been exposed as a myth. Ireland is a multi-cultured society, still struggling to live as the pluralist society it is.

The multi-faith dimension is also growing as ethnic minorities put down roots in Ireland. The process of globalisation impinges on consciousness and awareness grows of a world in which Christianity is a minority faith.

The last two decades have seen the acceleration of secularisation, which has meant the emergence of the cultural Catholic and secular Protestant. Meanwhile conflict dynamics continue in Northern Ireland and will not quickly go away, even with an agreed political settlement. The process of building peace will take decades.

The Church in any of its denominational expressions no longer has the guaranteed right to be heard. Only embodied integrity will win a hearing, not institutional authority. Embodied integrity can be developed through dialogue that has the capacity to listen as well as to speak.

To be Church in the multi-cultural context of the present is to engage in dialogue with a wide range of groups, identities and faiths, as well as with those claiming no faith identity. The listening aspect of dialogue will be ready to hear the questions.

John Howard Yoder wrote of reconciling dialogue 'with forgiveness and the discipline of conflict resolution'.[2] It is this spiritual and moral dimension that the Church can contribute to the peace process. Such a role will include the often excluded and will be the Church in a reconciling process.

4. Church as community of authentic transformation

The Church has been described as embodied in history and not a Gnostic idea above history.[3] To accept this is to avoid spiritualising the idea of Church and thus prevents an overemphasis on the invisible Church. It is also to take seriously the humanity of the Church or, as Luther saw it, a community at once forgiven yet sinful.

The role envisaged here is that of Church as faithful model for human community. It has been described as 'repenting and leading in following God's will on behalf of the whole society'.[4] This suggests the Church as an alternative community. It is a community of people following the way of God made known in Jesus Christ. It is in repenting and following that the Church models transformation and becomes a transformative presence in society. The Church as community of authentic transformation models 'what it means to live in love, justice, inclusiveness, servanthood, forgiveness – and confessing its own need for forgiveness'.[5] This also includes moral perceptiveness and critical awareness in relation to the social and political powers of society.

It is in its liturgies, catechetical and educational programmes that the Church will give substance to this model. These also may require significant change.

5. Church as ecumenical community

Notwithstanding the negative connotations that have been imposed on the word 'ecumenical' in sectors of Northern Ireland, and especially its being associated with a united Ireland agenda, the word still has rich biblical roots that need recovery. In its deepest sense, ecumenism is about world openness going beyond narrow parochialism and provincialism. It is often overlooked that all expressions of Christianity are culture-specific. That is unavoidable and even, to a point, necessary. But the culture-specific always needs to be relativised. When the culture-specific becomes the absolute or ultimate truth about God, then God is diminished and faith becomes introverted, if not sectarian.

The Church's task is always to open up, stretch and expand horizons and to challenge all local and denominational parochialism. Indeed, denominational or confessional traditions are becoming less and less meaningful in today's global experience. We may well be in a post-denominational, post-confessional age.

The Church is a 'universal community of redemption'.[6] This perspective opens the local faithful to a richer experience and vision of God. To move beyond sectarianism and sectarian versions of faith and God is to build and nurture a community of world openness, and that includes openness to other faith and ethical expressions. The Church as ecumenical community is to model openness to the universal Christian community and the rest of humanity with whom planet earth is shared. It is in the totality of these relationships that world peace depends.

Conclusion

Any future vision of Church in Ireland, as elsewhere, will include a plurality of models. The plurality will include the institutional model. The latter cannot be avoided no matter how much disillusionment there may be with the present institutional expressions. Community always requires organised and institutional forms, and always creates them. At the same time rich diverse expressions of Church are possible and desirable. The diversity requires unity. It is not enough to reduce Church to a variety of interest groups. The whole body of Christ needs to function with coherence and in unity. In a changing Ireland, renewal and transformation of Church is beginning to happen. The Holy Spirit, who can never be domesticated, tamed or imprisoned, is present for the renewal and reconciliation of community.

References

1. Peter C. Hodgson, *Winds of the Spirit: A Constructive Christian Theology* (Louisville, Kentucky: Westminister John Knox Press, 1994), p. 297.
2. Stassen, Yeager and Yoder, *Authentic Transformation: A New Vision of Christ and Culture* (Nashville: Abingdon Press, 1996), p. 209.
3. Ibid., p. 222.
4. Ibid., p. 233.
5. Ibid., p. 234.
6. Hodgson, op. cit., p. 303.

Questions

1. *Church as pilgrim community*

   'Faith as packaged, to be accepted or rejected is no longer where many are.' Is this true?

   If so, what are the implications?

   What would Church as pilgrim people look like?

2. *Church as public community*

   How does the Church show a concern for justice issues?

   What might a prophetic Church look like?

   How can the Church speak the truth to those in power?

   How does the Church build bridges with the local community and with wider society?

3. *Church as community of reconciling dialogue*

   How can the Church dialogue with a multi-cultured society?

   What else can the Churches do to be peacemakers in Northern Ireland?

4. *Church as community of authentic transformation*

   What would it mean for the Church to be an alternative community?

   What examples are there of alternative communities in Ireland that you know of?

5. *Church as ecumenical community*

   How can the Church be open to the world and yet rooted in the gospel?

   What are the limits to this openness? Might we lose our Christian identity?

   Does a Church have to be rooted in a culture or a national identity?

   Does that then make us sectarian? What are the relationships between Christ and culture, faith and nationalism, Church and politics?

VII

IMAGES OF THE CHURCH

Dr David Stevens

Various images are used for the Church. Some of these have already appeared in the previous paper, for example, Church as the body of Christ, Church as the people of God.

Some people use the image of Church as rock, or as fortress, or as 'fragile ark in a flood of hopelessness', or as 'colony of heaven' (Stanley Hauerwas) or as 'island' in which Christian discipleship is faithfully lived out. The image of Church as 'ideal society' has been utilised, as has that of 'light of the nations'. The lay theologian Anne Thurston has employed the image of the Church 'tented' among the pilgrim people. And so on.

Biblical images of the Church

There are various biblical images of the Church and we use material drawn from the World Council of Churches' Faith and Order paper, *The Nature and Purpose of the Church*, to reflect on these. Some of the images are images of stability and locality, some of mobility, some are more organic images, while others stress the relational character of the Church.

(a) Church as people of God

In the calling of Abraham, God was choosing for himself a holy people. The recalling of this election and vocation found frequent expression in the words of the prophets: 'I will be their God and they shall be my people' (Jer 31:33; Ez 37:27; Hos 2:23, echoed in 2 Cor 6:16; Heb 8:10). Through the Word (*dabhar*) of God and the Spirit (*rûàh*) of God, God chose and formed a people from among the nations to bring salvation to all. The election of Israel marked a decisive moment in the realisation of the plan of salvation. This covenant entails many things, including a calling to justice and truth. But it is also a gracious gift of *koinonia*, a dynamic impulse to communion which is evident throughout the story of the people of Israel, even when the community breaks *koinonia*. In the light of the ministry, teaching, and – above all – the death and resurrection of Jesus and the sending of the Holy Spirit at Pentecost, the Christian community believes that God sent his Son to bring the possibility of communion for people with each other and with God, thus manifesting the gift of God for the whole world.

In the Old Testament, the people of Israel are a pilgrim people journeying towards the fulfilment of the promise that in Abraham all the nations of the earth shall be blessed. In Christ this is fulfilled when, on the cross, the dividing wall between Jew and Gentile is broken down (Eph 2:14). Thus the Church, embracing Jew and Gentile, is a 'chosen race, a royal priesthood, a holy nation', 'God's own people' (1 Pet 2:9-10). The Church of God continues the way of pilgrimage to the eternal rest prepared for her (Heb 4:9-11). She is a prophetic sign of the fulfilment God will bring about through Christ by the power of the Spirit.

(b) Church as body of Christ

God's purpose was to reconcile humanity in one body, through the blood of Christ shed on the cross (Eph 2:11-22). This body is the body of Christ, the Church (Eph 1:23). Christ is the abiding head of this body and at the same time the one who, by the presence of the Spirit, gives life to it. Thus, Christ who is head of his body – empowering, leading and judging (Eph 5:23; Col 1:18) – is also one with it (1 Cor 12:12; Rom 12:5). The image of the body of Christ in the New Testament includes these two dimensions, one expressed in 1 Corinthians and Romans, the other developed in Ephesians.

It is through faith and baptism that human beings become members of the body of Christ (1 Cor 12:13). Through Holy

Communion, participation and communion in this body is renewed again and again (1 Cor 10:16). In being members of his body, Christians identify with the unique priesthood of Christ (Heb 9), and are called to live as faithful members: 'You are the holy priesthood' (1 Pet 2:9). Every member participates in the priesthood of the whole Church. No one exercises that priesthood apart from the unique priesthood of Christ, nor in isolation from the other members of the body.

All members of Christ are given gifts for the building up of the body (Rom 12:4-8; 1 Cor 12:4-30). The diversity and the specific nature of these gifts serve the Church's own life and its vocation as servant, so that God's kingdom in the world may be furthered.

According to the New Testament, it is through the Holy Spirit that human beings are baptised into the body of Christ (1 Cor 12:13). It is the same Holy Spirit who confers the manifold gifts to the members of the body (1 Cor 12:4, 7-11) and brings forth their unity (1 Cor 12). Thus, the image of 'body of Christ', though explicitly and primarily referring to the christological dimension of the Church, at the same time has deep pneumatological implications.

(c) Church as temple of the Holy Spirit

Reference to the essential relationship between Church and Holy Spirit runs through the whole New Testament witness. Nevertheless, there is no explicit image for this relationship. The imagery that comes particularly close is that of 'temple' and 'house'. This is so because the relation of the Spirit to the Church is one of indwelling, of giving life from within.

Built on the foundation of the apostles and prophets, the Church is God's household, a holy temple in which God lives by the Spirit. By the power of the Holy Spirit believers grow into 'a holy temple in the Lord' (Eph 2:21), into a 'spiritual house' (1 Pet 2:5). Filled with the Holy Spirit, Christians pray, love, work and serve in the power of the Spirit, leading a life worthy of their calling, eager to maintain the unity of the Spirit in the bond of peace (Eph 4:1-3).

(d) Other images

There are other images of the Church in the New Testament – most of them christological – like vine, flock, wedding party, bride. They all serve to highlight certain aspects of the Church's being and life: the vine image stresses its total dependence on Christ; the flock image stresses its trust and obedience; the party image stresses the eschatological reality of the Church; the bride image stresses the intimate though subordinate relation of the Church to Christ.

Questions
1. How do these various images of Church speak to us, for example, images of stability as opposed to mobility?
2. Do we favour images of stability in times of change? Why? Or images of mobility?
3. Does the particular image we favour reflect our pessimism about the world?
4. 'When we speak of "the church" we are not talking about anything other than the possibility of telling stories' (James Alison). These are the stories that capture the self-understanding of a faith community. How far do you think that this is true?

Koinonia (communion)

The term *koinonia* (communion) expresses the reality to which many of these biblical images refer – the nature and quality of the relationship of God's people to God and to one another. The basic verb from which the noun *koinonia* derives means 'to have something in common', 'to share', 'to participate', 'to have part in', 'to act together', or 'to be in a contractual relationship involving obligations of mutual accountability'. *Koinonia* is a notion rooted in the activity of the Holy Spirit as the action of God bringing unity and giving life to the body. It points to a Church community that is marked by a quality of relationships in and through which Jesus Christ is present.

As Alwyn Thomson says:

> The Christian community proclaims the gospel of God in its fullness and enacts the gospel in its life and practice. It is a body of people transformed by God. When true to their calling the people of God show that transformation in all of life – including political and social values and attitudes.[1]

Thus the Church seeks to demonstrate in its life the community and community-generating dimensions of God's love story with the universe.

Life for Christians in an increasingly secular society means a greater stress upon free personal faith and commitment. But it also means a corresponding recognition of the essentially communitarian nature of Christian faith.

Reference

1. Alwyn Thomson, *The Fractured Family* (Belfast: Evangelical Contribution on Northern Ireland, 1995), p. 22.

Questions
1. What are the signs of a Church marked by a quality of relationships in and through which Jesus Christ is present?
2. How can we promote authentic community in the Church?
3. How does an understanding of the Church as *koinonia* relate to those issues of ecclesiology that have divided the Churches?

CONTRIBUTORS

The Rev. Dr Johnston McMaster is a Methodist minister and Adult Education Lecturer for the Irish School of Ecumenics in Northern Ireland.

The Rev. Dr Trevor Morrow is Minister of Lucan Presbyterian Church, Dublin, and Moderator-designate of the Presbyterian Church in Ireland.

The Most Rev. Dr Leo O'Reilly is Roman Catholic Bishop of Kilmore.

Dr David Stevens is a Presbyterian layman and Joint Secretary of the Irish Inter-Church Meeting.

The Very Rev. Dr Stephen White is Church of Ireland Dean of Raphoe and author of *Authority and Anglicanism* (1996).

MEMBERS OF THE DEPARTMENT OF THEOLOGICAL QUESTIONS

Rev. Peter Donnelly
Rev. Feidhlimidh Magennis
Rev. Dr John Marsden
Rev. Dr Trevor Morrow
Very Rev. Michael Mullins
Rev. Professor Cecil McCullough
Sister Claire McGovern
Rev. Dr Johnston McMaster
Rev. Thomas O'Connor
Most Rev. Leo O'Reilly
Rev. David Steers
Rev. Oliver Treanor
Very Rev. Dr Stephen White

Secretariat

Sister Róisín Hannaway
Dr David Stevens

NOTES

NOTES

NOTES

NOTES

NOTES